Resource Activation

Christoph Flückiger, PhD, MAS Psychotherapy, is a member of the academic staff and a psychotherapist in the Department of Clinical Psychology and Psychotherapy at the University of Bern, Switzerland. He is also an instructor in several clinical training programs in Switzerland and Germany. Currently, he is an Honorary Fellow at the University of Wisconsin, Madison, WI, USA and at Northwestern University, Evanston, IL, USA. His research interests focus on understanding general mechanisms of change and how they can be implemented in daily practice.

Günther Wüsten, PhD, MAS Psychotherapy, is professor and program administrator of the training program in Psychosocial Counseling at the University of Applied Sciences in Olten, Switzerland. He also attended drama school in Zürich and was head of the Theater Department at the Cultural Center of Lübeck, Germany. He is interested in the processes of resource activation and self-regulation, particularly in the analysis of aims in life and motivation. He specializes in the instruction of role play in psychosocial counseling and psychotherapy.

Richard E. Zinbarg, PhD, is a professor in the Psychology Department of Northwestern University and in The Family Institute at Northwestern University, Evanston, IL, USA. He is currently an Associate Editor of the *Journal of Abnormal Psychology*. His research interests focus on understanding the structure and development of anxiety and depression, research methodology and basic measurement theory and techniques as well as treatments for anxiety disorders, with a particular focus on generalized anxiety disorder.

Bruce E. Wampold, PhD, ABPP, is Professor of Counseling Psychology at the University of Wisconsin, Madison, WI, USA. He is a Fellow of the American Psychological Association (APA, Divisions 12, 17, 29, 45), a Diplomate of the American Board of Professional Psychology, and a recipient of the APA Distinguished Professional Contributions to Applied Research Award. His current work involves understanding psychotherapy from empirical, historical, and anthropological perspectives, and is summarized in the volume *The Great Psychotherapy Debate: Models, Methods, and Findings*.

Resource Activation

Using Clients' Own Strengths in Psychotherapy and Counseling

Christoph Flückiger
Günther Wüsten
Richard E. Zinbarg
Bruce E. Wampold

Library of Congress Cataloging in Publication

is available via the Library of Congress Marc Database under the
LC Control Number 2009932406.

Library and Archives Canada Cataloguing in Publication

Resource activation: using clients' own strengths in psychotherapy and counseling /
Christoph Flückiger . . . [et al].
Translation of: Ressourcenaktivierung: Ein Manual für die Praxis.
Includes bibliographical references and index.
ISBN 978-0-88937-378-5

1. Psychotherapy.   2. Counseling.   3. Self-confidence.   I. Flückiger, Christoph, 1974–

RC480.R4713   2009   616.89'14   C2009-904389-0

The present volume is an adaptation of C. Flückiger & G. Wüsten, *Ressourcenaktivierung: Ein Manual für die Praxis*, published unter license from Verlag Hans Huber, Switzerland.

© 2010 by Hogrefe Publishing

PUBLISHING OFFICES

USA: Hogrefe & Huber Publishers, 875 Massachusetts Avenue, 7th Floor,
Cambridge, MA 02139, Phone (866) 823-4726, Fax (617) 354-6875;
E-mail customerservice@hogrefe-publishing.com

EUROPE: Hogrefe Publishing, Rohnsweg 25, 37085 Göttingen, Germany, Phone
+49 551 49609-0, Fax +49 551 49609-88, E-mail publishing@hogrefe.com

SALES & DISTRIBUTION

USA: Hogrefe Publishing, Customer Services Department, 30 Amberwood Parkway,
Ashland, OH 44805, Phone (800) 228-3749, Fax (419) 281-6883,
E-mail customerservice@hogrefe.com

EUROPE: Hogrefe Publishing, Rohnsweg 25, 37085 Göttingen, Germany, Phone
+49 551 49609-0, Fax +49 551 49609-88, E-mail publishing@hogrefe.com

OTHER OFFICES

CANADA: Hogrefe Publishing, 660 Eglinton Ave. East, Suite 119 – 514, Toronto,
Ontario M4G 2K2

SWITZERLAND: Hogrefe Publishing, Länggass-Strasse 76, CH-3000 Bern 9

Hogrefe Publishing. Incorporated and registered in the Commonwealth of Massachusetts, USA, and in Göttingen, Lower Saxony, Germany.

Printed and bound in the USA
ISBN: 978-0-88937-378-5

Foreword

The practice of psychotherapy and counseling is dedicated to helping individuals lead happier, more productive, and satisfying lives by helping to relieve the distress that motivated them to seek help. Thus, there is an emphasis on distress remediation: How can the therapist or counselor assist the client to address the issues that brought him or her to therapy? This perspective leads to a focus on problems and, in the extreme, to the development and dissemination of particular treatments for particular disorders. Efforts are made to alleviate the problem; if one conceptualizes the therapy process in a medical model, the goal is symptom reduction.

It is quite easy to be coerced or maybe even seduced into the medicalization of psychotherapy and counseling. In most contexts, we are now asked to provide diagnoses (*What disorder is being treated?*) and treatment plans (*How will the treatment address the symptoms of the disorder?*) to be reimbursed for services, or simply because it is required at the clinic or agency at which we work. Reading the academic journals, we see that they are focused on treatments for particular disorders – manuscripts on the topic of psychotherapy and counseling that do not investigate the treatment of a disorder have a low probability of being published in prestigious journals. And, of course, there is a push to remove psychological symptoms as quickly as possible, since most payers – whether government, managed care companies, or college administrations – require brief (as brief as possible) treatments for particular disorders.

As a result of the focus on brief treatments for disorders, it is understandable that counselors and therapists focus on client problems and the psychological bases of those problems. What is the client doing in his or her life that creates problems? How can I, the counselor or therapist, intervene to change destructive patterns? Simply put, great forces are being exerted to address distress.

It is not surprising then that we can easily forget that clients bring to therapy an immense array of strengths. Clients often have difficulties in a particular area (e.g., marital relationship) but are successful in others (e.g., their career). Even the most distressed and disadvantaged clients use their strengths to manage their own lives, despite having conditions that would frighten many of us. I am continually struck by the unrecognized courage that clients have to persevere through truly tough times. Some of us were trained in programs that emphasized client strengths and focused on client development, but it seems to me that the forces of the mental health services world are conspiring to work against using client strengths in therapy.

The dichotomy between remediation of symptoms and distress versus health and growth is a false one, however. Activating client resources by emphasizing strengths is not incompatible with distress remediation – it is simply a very positive and effective way to increase client well-being and reduce distress. Equally, focusing on strengths in therapy is not incompatible with existing treatments; incorporating therapeutic actions that utilize client strengths makes existing treatments more effective.

Resource Activation – Using Client's Own Strengths in Psychotherapy and Counseling provides pragmatic strategies that can be – or, rather, should be – used in therapy to help clients recognize and use their strengths. Sometimes therapeutic strategies involve simply changing the way we ask questions, focusing on coping and success rather than frustration and failures. Others involve more elaborate exercises to assist the client in recognizing and using their existing coping strategies, developing new strategies, and using their strengths. The questions, strategies, and exercises in this volume are deceptively simple, but often simple changes produce the best outcomes. However, a change of therapist attitude is needed – redirecting ourselves from a focus on symptoms and distress to a focus on client strengths.

Bruce E. Wampold, PhD, ABPP
University of Wisconsin – Madison

Table of Contents

Introduction

C. Flückiger, G. Wüsten, R.E. Zinbarg, and B.E. Wampold

Mr. M. has suffered from extreme shyness for many years now. He defines his current state as hopeless, and he has more or less given up thinking that he can learn to cope on his own. His shyness and his tendency toward social withdrawal have led to his losing nearly his entire circle of friends. He's been wanting a partner for years, but every time he sees an interesting woman, he freezes and can't even speak to her. When that happens, his negative cognitions of being the "most boring" man in the world simply overwhelm him. By the time these thoughts have receded, so has the chance of an encounter. These problems have assumed such a predominant position in Mr. M.'s life that he cannot think of anything else or do the things he most enjoys. Recently, however, he mustered the courage to look for professional help.

Mr. M. noticed that his therapist does not simply examine his symptoms, but rather also wants to understand his talents. His therapist, for instance, was very interested in Mr. M.'s job as a teacher and in his popularity with his pupils. Up to that point, Mr. M. had nearly forgotten how many interests he had. This in turn gives Mr. M. the confidence that he is indeed getting competent help – and the hope that his problems can be solved. With the help of the therapist, he tries to strengthen his innate but dormant talents and to build on his strengths and wishes to create new behavioral patterns. After seeing how the detailed work with his therapist has helped him make progress, Mr. M. gains the certainty that his state of affairs can be changed, which in turn motivates him to continue the therapy even more and to work on himself and his problems.

All of which is easier said than done! This manual is meant for psychologists, psychiatrists, social workers, supervisors, and counselors to illustrate practical starting points for directly diagnosing an individual's resources and employing them in therapy. It is written in an easy and relaxed style, using everyday language, to enable direct integration into therapy.

Counselors often find themselves in situations in which they have to make quick decisions about how to move forward without necessarily knowing in advance the possible solutions at their disposal. To find their way among these possibilities they need effective metastrategies for searching and finding heuristics that allow them to be able to react to the situation at hand (Groner, Groner, & Bischof, 1983). A central role is played by the way they handle the individual resources of the person seeking help. When trying to solve problems, one runs the risk of relegating a person's resources to the back burner by focusing solely on problematic aspects – which effectively assumes the negative cognitions of the person seeking help and leaves patients in their web of negative thoughts (Grawe, 1997, 2004). Upon starting therapy or counseling, people seeking help often feel hopeless and have given up believing in their own problem-solving resources. It is therefore the counselor's job to reactivate the experience of that person's self-effectiveness. A counselor should pick up on the person's existing strengths and skills.

The present manual illustrates how to actively take a person's resources into consideration during the therapy and counseling sessions, and how to integrate them into existing intervention concepts. This does not mean excluding a person's problematic aspects; on the contrary, a situation favorable to establishing a stronger resource orientation will simultaneously make a direct handling of the problems easier.

The first part illustrates several perspectives that can be used to focus attention on diagnostics and dialog, and that shed light on a person's individual resources from various angles. These therapeutic perspectives can be used in the framework of existing manuals and guidelines to focus on how to "do things." The second part illustrates procedures offering an adequate framework for further applying the different perspectives. The interventions illustrated here, of course, do not purport to be complete.

Further Reading

Flückiger, C., Caspar, F., Grosse Holtforth, M., & Willutzki, U. (2009). Working with the patients' strengths: A microprocess approach. *Psychotherapy Research, 19*, 213–223.

Flückiger, C., & Grosse Holtforth, M. (2008). Focusing the therapist's attention on the patient's strengths – A preliminary study to foster a mechanism of change in outpatient psychotherapy. *Journal of Clinical Psychology, 64*, 876–890.

Gassmann, D., & Grawe, K. (2006). General change mechanisms. The relation between problem activation and resource activation in successful and unsuccessful therapeutic interactions. *Journal of Clinical Psychology and Psychotherapy, 13*, 1–11.

Grawe, K. (1997). Research-informed psychotherapy. *Psychotherapy Research, 7*, 1–19.

Grawe, K. (2004). *Psychological therapy.* Seattle, WA: Hogrefe & Huber.

Grawe, K. (2006). *Neuropsychotherapy.* Mahwah, NJ: Erlbaum.

These two books offer, in a nutshell, an overall concept for psychotherapeutic modes of operation. They provide practical assistance for putting into context processes active in the interaction between patient and therapist and for influencing them therapeutically.

Smith, E., & Grawe, K. (2003). What makes psychotherapy sessions productive? A new approach to bridging the gap between process research and practice. *Clinical Psychology and Psychotherapy, 10,* 275–285.

Smith, E., & Grawe, K. (2005). Which therapeutic mechanisms works when? A step toward the formulation of empirically validated guidelines for therapists' session-to-session decisions. *Clinical Psychology and Psychotherapy,* 12, 112–123.

Willutzki, U., & Koban, C. (2004). Enhancing motivation for psychotherapy: The elaboration of positive perspectives (EPOS). In W.M. Cox & E. Klinger (Eds.), *Handbook of motivational counseling. Concepts, approaches and assessments.* West Sussex: Wiley.

Note: We make a point of using gender-neutral language in this volume, employing either neutral terms of reference or masculine and feminine terms at random.

1 Systematic Resource Analysis

C. Flückiger and G. Wüsten

Systematic resource analysis serves to complement existing case conceptions as presently used in therapy and counseling (e.g., situation analyses and relationship analyses). Resource analysis, illustrated in Figure 1-1, can be used both for training or for self-teaching.

Both in professional and private contexts we constantly form hypotheses about our counterparts – the way they behave, what they are thinking, what they care about, what makes them uncomfortable, and of course how they relate to us. We may have a more or less conscious image of the other person, and that image may be more or less influenced by our subjective impression.

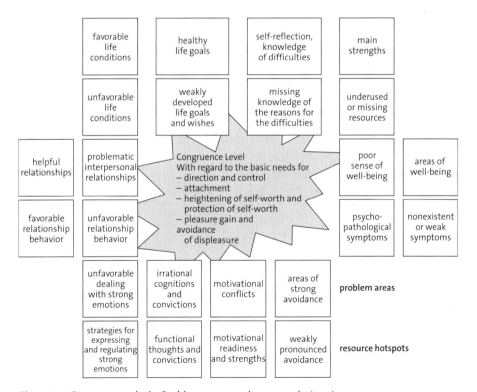

Figure 1-1. Resource analysis: Problem areas and resource hotspots.

Such an image can be solely problem-centered, thus neglecting that person's resources (Rosenhan, 1973; Duckworth, Steen, & Seeligman, 2005).

However, parallel to the diagnosis of "problems," it is possible to look for "resources" in the various areas of life. Often people have problems in certain areas of life and desperately try to solve them without realizing that they possess skills and talents that could be used toward achieving their goals. Figure 1-1 offers an overview of different areas of psychological functioning concerning both talents and skills as well as problems and difficulties. Areas with particularly helpful talents and skills we've denoted as "resource hotspots." One can determine the individual areas through direct questioning or more systematically through professional psychodiagnostics. We do not recommend a particular set of questionnaires because in our experience even the more traditional questionnaires allow one to determine relevant resources, and a useful combination thereof would differ depending on the institutional background. Obtaining an outside assessment from a close third party can sometimes prove extremely beneficial because the person seeking help may be unaware of their own resources.

Resource hotspots are sources of contentment and well-being. The consistency principle says that people are happy only when their needs and respective goals are consistent, and when they can attain "personal goals." On the one hand, resources are the means a person uses to achieve such goals; on the other hand, the goals themselves contribute to the satisfaction of basic needs. According to Grawe (1998, 2004) possible basic needs are as follows:

1) The need for bonding, for experiencing close relationships and friendships;
2) The need for direction and control, to know one's scope of action;
3) The need for a higher sense of self-value;
4) The need to gain pleasure and avoid displeasure.

Before you develop solutions on your own, you should gain a broad understanding of a person's individual resources. Table 1-1 lists a few examples of appropriate questions.

Table 1-1. Possible questions for examining individual resources in different areas of psychological functioning

Favorable life conditions (client and significant other)	What areas in the individual's past and current professional and personal life are considered satisfying?
Healthy life goals	What are the individual's attainable goals, life plans, and wishes?
Self-reflection, knowledge of one's own difficulties	Can the person reflect on his or her own problems? Does the person have a sense of how the problems arose?
Special skills	Does the person have particular skills that stand out from those of others?
Areas of well-being	Does the person have positive memories? In what areas of life has the individual felt comfortable?
Nonexistent or weak symptoms	Where has the complete psychopathological picture not been reached? How pronounced are the symptoms? What caused the situation to worsen?
Weakly pronounced avoidance	Is avoidance behavior limited to certain places, times, or moods?
Motivational readiness and strengths	Does the person show positive motivations such as social integration, connectedness with others, or high productivity?
Functional cognitions and conviction	Do positive thoughts and convictions exist that make it easier to face difficult situations?
Expression and regulation potential for strong emotions	To what extent can the person verbalize and self-regulate emotions?
Favorable relationship behavior	To what extent can the person enter into relationships? What is necessary for this to happen?
Helpful relationships	Does the person have friends and people who can be trusted? Were there any such relationships in the past?

1.1 Resource Priming

Resource priming is a systematic way for counselors to prepare by making them focus more on the resources of the person seeking help (see Worksheet 1 in the Appendix). It helps implement resource analysis in therapy and counseling. Figure 1-2 shows an example of resource priming.

Resource priming is best done at the beginning of a course of therapy or counseling in order to flow into the first few sessions. It would be ideal if the counselor were to focus on the resource hotspots and find a way of putting them to good use in the upcoming session. This revisualization of the patient's resources is meant to facilitate the change of perspective.

Column 1: First of all, the individual resource hotspots that resulted from resource analysis and were explored in the initial conversation are collated. It is important to formulate a workable number of resource hotspots, subsuming individual resource areas in main categories. If in the course of the sessions new additional crucial hotspots are found, these can be documented as well under the heading "Additional resources over the course of the therapy."

By collating resource hotspots, the counselor, after a few initial problems, may in the end think of so many different resources that the impression arises

Resource hotspots		How can they be activated?		How well was the resource activated?*				
Test battery/clinical impression	I	Within therapy	Outside of therapy	1	2	3	4	5
Married for 51 years	1	Wife as expert on the patient's problems and strengths	Mutual activities	4	3	3	2	2
Vivid storyteller	3	Notice, estimate	Local pub and friends at the camping site	3	3	3	1	3
Self-definition as a foreman	2	Therapy as hard work, tackling things	Personal project	4	0	0	3	1
Additional resources over the course of the therapy								
Long-time GP	4		Same understanding of problems		1	0		4

Notes: I = assessment of the *importance* for the patient; *assessment after the sessions 1–5: 4 = extremely, 3 = very, 2 = fairly, 1 = somewhat, 0 = not at all.

Figure 1-2. Example of the resource priming of a 72-year-old clinically depressed patient.

that the individual possesses many more resources than the average patient –
a first indication of the change of perspective.

Column 2: After formulating the resource hotspots, rank these according to
the importance of crucial needs. The explicitly motivational meaning of an
action is often hard for the observer to recognize, although one can usually
assess the importance of the action to the person carrying it out.

Column 3 and *Column 4*: After creating a ranking of important resource hotspots, look for ways to activate the resource hotspots both during sessions
and outside of sessions. The goal is to find as many ways of activation as
possible. The resource hotspots can be activated independently of the problem areas in question; on the other hand, they can also be useful when working through distinct problems. It is vital to document everything, even things
taken for granted because otherwise they could be neglected.

Column 5 to *Column 9*: Following the sessions, assess the extent to which the
individual resource hotspots were activated in the session.

2 Resource-Oriented Dialog Strategies

C. Flückiger, G. Wüsten, and R.E. Zinbarg

Manuals or guidelines tend to focus on the description of certain therapeutic or counseling methods – on "what" to do. Often, "how" it is done is overhastily shrugged off as clear and thus negligible. The following chapter offers an overview of several strategies of resource-oriented dialog that can be used to channel the individual's attention. Think of it as moving and focusing a source of light or as a resource that can be looked at from various angles. These perspectives are characterized by opposite poles, whereby the two poles of a perspective are in fact complementary.

The job of the counselor is to focus the attention on one or the other pole of a single resource perspective during the session. Patient are often in a state in which they tend to focus on their deficits and are largely unaware of their resources. In order to further an active change of perspective, the counselor has to break out of the patient's thinking patterns.

The goal of resource-oriented dialog is to heighten the patient's immediate positive emotional experience and thus to make it easier for that person to work through problems. Progressive integration of the resource perspective sets a positive feedback mechanism in motion, characterized by an improved working relationship as well as greater openness and cooperation: It reactivates one's own attempts at coping with the problem. In friendly discussions with family or friends resource-oriented dialog often occurs spontaneously and is recognized as such only when it is missing. Discussions are then perceived as halting and slow.

It is possible to differentiate between the following perspectives with two opposing poles:

1) Perceiving and validating *directly available resources* and actively searching out *unused resources*.
2) *Verbalizing resources* and immediately *experiencing resources*.
3) Using *potential resources* and integrating *motivational resources*.

4) Strengthening *personal resources* and furthering the *available resources* of the *social network*.

5) Focusing on *problem-independent resources* and taking advantage of *problem-relevant resources*.

6) Optimizing *usable resources* and boosting and maintaining *trainable resources*.

In the following, we explain the individual resource perspectives and point out relevant questions. Short case studies serve to exemplify the change of perspective from a deficit-oriented one to a resource-oriented one. In contrast, an intervention is always presented that remains stuck in a deficit-oriented perspective. We are not suggesting that these questions are not pertinent; rather, we wish to emphasize the technical aspect of the change of perspective. A resource that is not picked up is not necessarily a "wasted opportunity," but can be discussed at a later stage.

2.1 Perceiving and Validating Directly Available Resources and Actively Introducing Unused Resources

Perceiving and Validating Directly Available Resources

At first sight it might seem trivial, but recognizing a directly available resource is the result of a complex calculation within a means-ends model in which the counselor has recognized the goals, the potential means of attaining those goals as well as the function of available resources. Available resources can be so self-evident that the counselor is not even aware of them. Or they might be so "minor" as to prove useful at some later stage and are simply denoted for later use. And they can be the first small changes and improvements that can then be explored in more detail.

Possible questions:
- Have I sufficiently attended to the unproblematic results of the questionnaire?
- Are there any changes or improvements?
- Have I adequately reinforced behavior useful to therapy?
- What is the patient's contribution by coming to the session?

Case Study

Ms. H.: I know that my difficulties with my husband have a lot to do with my past.
Deficit-oriented intervention: Where do you see your contribution to the problems with your husband?
Resource-oriented intervention: You have the ability to reflect on the difficulties you're experiencing with your husband and connect them with yourself and your own past. Where do you see a connection?

Actively Introducing Unused Resources

Unused resources are tools the person has employed in the past but does not actively use any more. Perhaps he or she has not practiced using these tools in a while or has had some negative experiences in connection with them, or can no longer use them to the same extent.

Introducing unused resources requires a careful approach: On the one hand, the solution strategy of the therapist or counselor may be too simple, and on the other hand, the client must have enough faith.

Possible questions:
- Does the person have skills they didn't think of in the case in question?
- Does the person have skills they do not feel confident using?
- Were there exceptions in the past?
- Were there exceptions in other areas?
- Has a step been taken in the right direction?

Case Study

Mr. H.: When my wife bosses me around, I just tell myself: "Silence is golden." I do it just to keep the peace.
Deficit-oriented intervention: So you avoid a confrontation with your wife?
Resource-oriented intervention: Were there any other similar situations in the past in which you reacted differently?

2.2 Verbalizing Resources and Immediately Experiencing Resources

Verbalizing Resources

The advantage of talking openly about resources is that the resource becomes explicitly and consciously applicable. It can be assumed that the resource has a motivational background and is thus a source of information for greater motivational goals. Being aware of the exemplary significance of a person's specific resource can give you access to what matters in that person's life and to the tools they use to attain their motivational goals.

Resource-oriented dialog strategies can happen indirectly, convoluted in subordinate clauses. The counselor can point out what the person is particularly good at, what changes they have gone through, or what they can be proud of

Possible questions:
– Can I picture in my mind the resource the person is describing to me?
– Have I understood the subjective significance of the resource for the person?
– What is the influence of the person's "beaming" when they tell the story?
– Can I casually suggest a resource by the way?

Case Study

Mr. M.: No really, I like playing soccer in a team!
Deficit-oriented intervention: How often did you make the team, then?
Resource-oriented intervention: That's great, and what is it you particularly enjoy?

Immediately Experiencing Resources

By discussing resources in depth the person may directly experience their resources *in sensu*. Experiencing them immediately does not necessarily mean verbalizing them, however: The ideal scenario would be for the person to find a way of working through them in which they see themselves as particularly competent, for instance, by keeping a tidy diary, precise computer graphics, or efficient notes. In addition, experiencing problem-free areas can be a relief in and of itself.

Possible questions:
- What does the patient enjoy and how can I integrate it into the way we are working through the problem?
- How can I adapt the process to the person's skills?
- To what extent can I adapt to the person's own "living space" without giving him or her the impression that I am pandering (language, metaphors, non-verbal cues)?

Case Study

Mr. K.: It's really hard to fill out this worksheet.

Deficit-oriented intervention: Yes, I can imagine how that would be a difficult task for you. Still, I think it's important for you to stick with it.

Resource-oriented intervention: Yes, it is really hard. What do you think made you stick with it nevertheless?

2.3 Using Potential Resources and Integrating Motivational Resources

Using Potential Resources

Potential resources are existing or unused skills and talents one ascribes to oneself. When potential resources are activated, the person perceives themselves to be active and capable of accomplishing things. Potential resources are the tools employed by the person to achieve their goals.

Possible questions:
- What is the person particularly good at?
- What comes natural to them?
- When does the person start to "flow"?

Case Study

Ms. S.: I can barely manage to get through the day, with my little daughter's screaming, my job situation, and an ex who doesn't pay any child support – it's just too much!
Deficit-oriented intervention: Perhaps you are taking on too much at the moment?
Resource-oriented intervention: It seems to me you manage a lot of troubles at the moment!

Integrating Motivational Resources

On the one hand, motivational resources are consciously represented goals, wishes, and decisions the person feels committed to; on the other hand, they are motivational schemata and biographically acquired plans used by the person more or less consciously to satisfy basic needs. Motivational resources are, to use an image, the carrots dangling in front of the rabbit that cause him to continue (Caspar, 2007).

Possible questions:
- What are the individual's life dreams?
- What idols does the individual have?
- In what areas does the person have positive expectations of change?
- What really matters to the person?

Case Study

D.: I want to be a famous popstar, I don't need to understand math.
Deficit-oriented intervention: But to be famous, you first have to achieve something.
Resource-oriented intervention: What about when you're famous and can't trust anyone, then you'll have to do all the math yourself.

2.4 Strengthening Personal Resources and Furthering the Available Resources of the Social Network

Strengthening Personal Resources

Personal resources are characteristics, dispositions, traits, skills, and talents used by the individual to satisfy their basic needs. These resources are, on the one hand, personal because the individual can use them at will; on the other hand, the individual feels capable of applying them to attain their goals.

Possible questions:
– What get the person excited?
– What does the person feel committed to?
– What leaves them cold? And why?

Case Study

Mr. M.: If my company goes bankrupt, then I'm responsible for the failure.
Deficit-oriented intervention: Bankruptcy is dependent on a number of different factors.
Resource-oriented intervention: Free enterprise implies the courage to take risks.

Furthering the Available Resources of the Social Network

People are generally not all-powerful within their social network; they are, however, also not completely at the mercy of that network. Rather, in many areas of life they possess a certain measure of power. Many needs can be satisfied only by being with other people. The social network can include the individual's partner, their family, a best friend, acquaintances from work or leisure activity, a circle of friends or neighborhood acquaintances. Social contexts can be described on many different levels, from individual relationships to one's socio-economic and cultural context. The breadth of this area should not deter the counselor from looking impartially for all possible resources.

Possible questions:
– Is there a strong role model in the family or circle of friends?
– Where can the patient count on social support?

- Is there someone the patient trusts?
- What setting is particularly suited from a resource perspective (individual, couple, family, group)?

Case Study

Mr. G.: I often feel very lonely, except for one friend. I hardly ever meet up with anybody.

Deficit-oriented intervention: You often feel lonely and hardly ever meet anyone?

Resource-oriented intervention: What do you and your friend have in common?

2.5 Focusing on Problem-Independent Resources and Taking Advantage of Problem-Relevant Resources

Focusing on Problem-Independent Resources

Problem-independent resources are areas in which an individual sees themselves as unproblematic or untouched by problems. These areas can be connected to leisure and encompass favorite pastimes, hobbies, passions, etc. They are also often connected with interpersonal resources. Collecting stamps, for instance, can be an opportunity for (interpersonal) exchange.

Possible questions:
– When does the patient see themselves as unproblematic?
– Where does the individual derive pleasure?
– How does the individual find peace and relax?
– Were there any good times in the past?
– Did I take the time to allow the patient to rave about their passions?

Case Study

Ms. K.: In the light of my current job situation, my vacation was like being on furlough from prison.
Problem-oriented intervention: What influence did your job situation have on your vacation?
Resource-oriented intervention: What aspects of your vacation had a particularly beneficial effect?

Taking Advantage of Problem-Relevant Resources

Problem-relevant resources are conditions that make it easier to work through problematic aspects. Often the person sees their problems as a bottomless pit or as completely impenetrable. Problem-relevant resources are tied to the problems and define them.

Possible questions:
– To what extent can the problem be delimited in terms of content and time?
– Are there exceptions?

– What caused the situation to change for the better?
– To what extent is the problem understood and to what extent can I validate that?

Case Study

Mr. W.: For me it's like a huge mountain in front of me, and I don't know how to face it.

Problem-oriented intervention: Do you feel stressed out and blocked at the moment?

Resource-oriented intervention: Is it possible that the mountain appears bigger to you than it actually is?

2.6 Optimizing Usable Resources and Boosting and Maintaining Trainable Resources

Like problems, resources are not unlimited. The last perspective focuses on maintaining existing resources and preventing a quick-fix attitude.

Optimizing Usable Resources

Material resources are finite, time is precious, a relationship bonus can dry up. The resources we use come at a price and can have side effects. And they can be used wastefully or carelessly or not to their full advantage.

Possible questions:
- Can the quality of a resource be maintained?
- How far can you go before exhausting a resource?
- What are the limits of a usable resource?
- Is the cost-benefit ratio still valid?

Case Study

Ms. T: Since I started working as a flight attendant, with the irregular working hours that entails, I have been seeing my friends less and less.
Problem-oriented intervention: Are you perhaps neglecting your friends?
Resource-oriented intervention: Your friends seem to mean a great deal to you. How can you maintain a good relationship with your friends despite spending less time together?

Boosting and Maintaining Trainable Resources

Trainable resources are talents and skills that have to be practiced and worked at. "Use it or lose it" is true for many areas of cultural and intellectual life as well. Interestingly, trainable resources often act according to the saying: "To those who have, more shall be given." Trainable resources create conditions that maintain existing environments and open up new ones.

Possible questions:
- Have I repeated what I have learned enough?
- Is regularity a sensible thing?
- Is there potential for variation?

Case Study

Mr. R: I can afford not to exercise for 6 months because basically I'm a very athletic person. This gives me the chance to study more effectively for my exam.

Problem-oriented intervention: Is it important to you to have enough time to learn for your exam?

Resource-oriented intervention: It seems to me you might be stealing from Peter to Paul.

2.7 Perspectives as Heuristics for Directing Attention

The six perspectives mentioned above function as search-and-find heuristics, allowing the person to move inside the complex solution space and look for potential solution paths. The heuristics are hence not precise algorithms in a clearly delineated problem-solving space. If all six perspectives are combined together with two poles, we then have a table consisting of 64 squares on which every single resource can be located.

If a therapist encourages a patient with a fear of public speaking to give a talk, an immediate (2.1), personal (2.3), motivational (2.4), problem-relevant (2.5), trainable (2.6) resource has been verbalized (2.2). This division has little practical use, however, because an individual possesses many different resources, and because even the most disparate resources are contained within resource hotspots. Thus, it is important to have simple meta-strategies that allow the counselor to maintain an overview of things.

Worksheet 2 (see Appendix) offers an overview of the six resource-oriented perspectives and the respective questions. The aim of these perspectives is to direct attention during therapy and the counseling process in the short term.

Paying compliments and expressing praise can happen in many ways. Humor can be dry, supported by wild gestures, benign, or vitriolic. It is influenced among other things by cultural values and mores. The dark humor that can help two Scots to bond may be hurtful to others. What seems genuine to one person may appear fake to another. Like humor, resource-oriented dialog is created through the interaction of two interlocutors. It is not dependent solely on the patient/client, but is rather influenced by the counselor's preferences and fears as well.

For training and self-study purposes, we suggest that you focus first on a single perspective and exhaust it in a counseling and therapy session and then rotate different perspectives. By practicing the perspectives systematically, you will train your perception, i.e., your ability to observe the therapy and counseling process from a specific angle, while at the same time boosting your flexibility, i.e., your ability to take on different perspectives during the entire process.

2.8 Resource-Orientation – Putting the Cart Before the Horse

When building new behavioral patterns, the individual goes through several phases of planning and carrying out the course of action. In general, it is possible to single out four phases (Gollwitzer & Schaal, 2001):

1) In the *choice phase*, different goals are weighed out, and the pros and cons are studied. Eventually, a decision is made in favor of a goal, the Rubicon is crossed and the die is cast.
2) In the *planning phase*, the course of action is planned, decisions are made with regard to their implementation, and the necessary tools are chosen. At the end of this phase a choice is made as to when, where, and how the action will be carried out.
3) The *action phase* follows, the conduct of which is monitored and shielded from external influences. This phase ends with the completion of the action.
4) In the final *evaluation phase*, the action is reviewed and evaluated (see Figure 2-1).

In order to build new behavioral patterns, these four phases have to be passed through systematically from beginning to end. In that respect it is vital that the counselor not be forced to move to the next phase without giving the preceding phase the complete attention it requires. For instance, an alcoholic might go to rehab without having dealt with the all pros and cons of the changes that might occur. This model has proven extremely beneficial in terms of building new behavioral patterns.

We agree wholeheartedly with this position, but would like also to point out that what is available should be used as befits the situation. Just as new

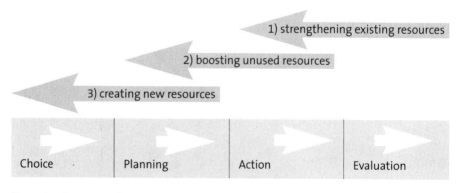

Figure 2-1. Resource orientation in the general action model.

behavioral patterns have to be built up from the very beginning, existing unproblematic dispositions and decisions have to be used starting from the end point and moving backwards:

1) Existing resources have to be strengthened and maintained.
2) Unused resources have to be boosted and revived.
3) New resources have to be created.

2.9 Differences in Self- and Other-Perception

An individual's self- and other-perception do not necessarily agree. What is vital to the counselor is to know the patient's perception from which different interventions can be deduced. If an object is seen by both patient and counselor as a resource, it can also be strengthened and boosted; if the counselor identifies a resource that is not recognized as such by the patient, it is the counselor's duty to introduce the resource *gently*. If it is the counselor who does not agree with the evaluation of the positive resource, he or she should point out the problematic aspects of that resource. And if, finally, something is considered problematic by both sides, its significance and importance can be explored, validated, and potentially defined (see Table 2-1).

Table 2-1. Overview of self- and other-perception of resources and the respective task

		Patient/client	
		Resource	No resource
Therapist/counselor	Resource	Strengthening/mentioning	Introducing
	No resource	Resolving	Validating/defining

2.10 Problem Situation and Therapeutic Strategies

Resource orientation is dependent on how well the patient has handled the problem. Depending on how aware the patient is of the problem, different resource-oriented interventions will be suitable. As in a means-ends model, three different problem situations and therapeutic strategies can be singled out (see Figure 2-2):

1) *Problem situation:* Problems are known, goals are unproblematic, and means are clear.
   Therapeutic strategies: It is the counselor's duty to support the patient's intent by maintaining, strengthening, or helping to build potential resources. This happens, for instance, when the counselor points out personal strengths and talents, reinforces positive feelings or interpersonal skills, and emphasizes positive expectations of change, and attends to the progress being made.
2) *Problem situation:* Problems are known, but goals and/or means are unclear.
   Therapeutic strategies: It is the counselor's job to strengthen or reinforce the patient's motivational resources. The counselor helps the patient to verbalize goals, to visualize solutions, and to substantiate them – as well as to find a balance of goals between means and finally to come to a decision.
3) *Problem situation:* Problems, goals, and means are unclear.
   Therapeutic strategies: It is the counselor's job to gain an overview of the patient's situation (see Chapter 1) and to narrow down the problems so as to

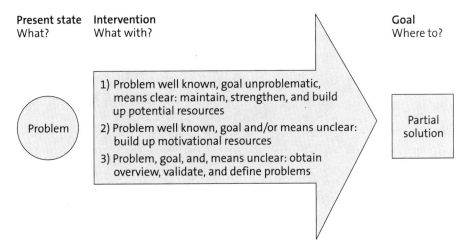

Figure 2-2. Problem situation and appropriate resource-oriented interventions.

make them appear more manageable to the patient. The counselor can normalize the problems ("You're not alone with your problems"), point to downward comparisons ("How could it get worse?"), work out exceptions ("Are or were there situations when the problem is/was less pronounced?") and reassess problems positively (for reframing, see Chapter 3.10).

Counselors and therapists are often a few steps ahead of their patient without even being aware of it. The inherent danger is that the counselor encourages the patient to take a step before the conditions for it are in place. For instance, they may emphasize an individual's potential resources for the attainment of their goals (solution strategy 1) before the person knows exactly what goals they would like to achieve (problem situation 2). The therapist has fallen prey to a quick-fix attitude.

2.11 Resource-Oriented Strategies and Phases of Therapy

Resource activation as a curative factor in psychotherapy and counseling draws on the individual's strengths and qualities that can be applied in the service of (therapeutic) goals. People seeking help often feel hopeless when they start therapy or counseling, and have often given up believing in their own problem-solving capacities. Revitalizing the person's own coping strategies is therefore a central goal at the beginning of a therapy. Resource-oriented strategies have various therapeutic functions depending on the phase of therapy (Howard, Lueger, Maling, & Martinovich, 1993).

First phase (remoralization): Fostering preexisting resources, reactivation of formerly invested resources, and building up of new resources:
– Assessing resources
– Estimating and validating preexisting strengths
– Integrating individual strengths into the case formulation
– Using positive expectations
– Consolidating therapy motivation and motivation to change
– Inducing hope
– Setting up a therapeutic alliance based on strengths and problems
– Analyzing early gains
– Promoting self-efficacy and control expectations
– Isolating patient problems

Middle phase of therapy (remediation): Facilitating approach to problem by making individual resources apparent:
– Reinforcing patient's active participation in therapeutic work
– Working out a rationale based on individual strengths
– Using successful coping strategies
– Using successful problem solving strategies
– Choosing (therapeutic) interventions that conform to the patient's preexisting strengths
– Intensifying problem approach by validating preexisting capabilities and goals
– Fostering acceptance of unalterable constraints by pointing out existing strengths

End of therapy (rehabilitation): Consolidation and development of new behaviors
- Consolidating newly acquired skills
- Fostering the transfer and extension of these skills to other situations
- Boosting well-being
- Maintaining resiliency
- Fostering self-effiacy, self-esteem, and autonomy

2.12 Risks and Side Effects of Resource-Oriented Strategies

Therapists and counselors often voice the fear that too emphatic praise may be perceived as flattery. But this is not necessarily the case. In a study we carried out ourselves, of the 6247 minutes we monitored, trained external observers rated the resource activation as excessive in only 6 minutes – even when the trained therapists were instructed to maximize resource activation.

The following difficulties could arise:
- Resource analysis is no substitute for a personalized case formulation (Chapter 1).
- Often solutions seem simple and obvious, prompting the counselor to strive to implement them as quickly as possible. Don't! Problems may be misunderstood, and solutions may end up being imposed on the patient (Chapter 2.9).
- Any resource activation coming as an afterthought following a difficult therapy session and beginning with the word "but" may be perceived as appeasement. Resource activation has to be integrated into the therapy and counseling process at an early stage and then progressively extended – and not tacked on of an afterthought in an act of self-exoneration.
- Goals can be too ambitious so that the difference between the state actually experienced and the desired state can be too large. This can lead to resistance or frustration.
- Extreme praise of something that is a matter of course can be perceived as patronizing. Example: "It's great of you to always be exactly on time for our session, Mr. Swatch!"
- The counselor tries desperately to build up new resources instead of using existing ones (Chapter 2.8).
- The counselor strengthens problem behavior by not paying enough attention to the problematic aspects of a resource. For instance, assertiveness present in an antisocial person is not automatically a resource (Chapter 2.10).
- "That's easy for you to say! You're a therapist!" Don't let this answer irritate you. Here is a possible response: "Of course I'm a therapist. What is central, however, is how you feel about this."

3 Resource-Activating Structural Interventions

G. Wüsten and C. Flückiger

In the following we describe therapeutic interventions that can engender whole chains of resource activations and structure sessions. Drawing up a life overview can take up a whole session, and even miracle questions, working out goals, or preparing a imagination require a certain amount of time. As with all interventions, the only sensible ones are those that tie in with the clients' skills and motivational dispositions. For instance, visualization is not right for every person undergoing therapy. Moreover, resource-oriented structural interventions can also be carried out in a very deficit-oriented way. The methods work depends on the specific case conditions and institutional framework. Structural interventions offer particularly good prerequisites for directing the person's attention to their resources and deepening them.

3.1 Life Overview

In order to create an environment that is simultaneously comfortable and structured, working out a life overview can prove beneficial. The goal is to understand the development of both the client's problems and resources. It is important to find – in collaboration with the patient/client – a coherent explanation for their problems on the basis of their life experiences. And yet resources have to be constantly monitored. Particularly positive life events are stressed from this angle and probed in more depth through relevant questions: "Can you please tell me about this event in more detail? What were you feeling when that was happening? What were others thinking about you? How exactly did you achieve that? How do you feel today having experienced the event?"

Procedure

The initial phase of psychotherapy or counseling is fundamentally well-suited to the creation of a life overview. A life overview contains important events of an individual's life. Life events are recorded on several overlapping timelines, which form thematic focal points. Education/schooling, family life, important relationships, and romantic relationships have proved useful. Depending on the particular situation, additional timelines can be created for specific themes, e.g., travel, health issues, etc. When the timelines are discussed, the therapist should be able to visualize the situation at a specific point in time. Although the topics themselves may seem banal, it is not a matter of asking standard questions; rather, it is vital that the resource perspective dictate the questions. In the case of education and schooling, for example, the questions might be: "What were your favorite subjects?," "Did you have a favorite teacher?," "What did you like about them?," "What did you learn about them?," "What was your relationship with other pupils?," "If you had to define your role, how would you characterize it?"

The counselor tries to find anchor points in the biography which can be coupled with schema activation. In the context of the questions mentioned above, difficulties may arise and problems may come to the fore. Those difficult experiences should not be suppressed or negated. Yet is also important not to get stuck in difficult problems, but rather to gain a complete overview, so that both negative and positive events can find their place within the overview. The acknowledged presence of both sides alone can lead to an expansion of the patient's consciousness.

One simple way to ensure this is to make sure the life overview starts off with some everyday aspect of life (e.g., education/schooling). Later the counselor can gain a broader overview of the patient's situation. In addition, the level of discussion can be deepened through the use of "how" questions.

The overview can also be recorded on a flip chart, which makes the information readily available to both partners. Over the course of the work, a full picture will emerge, structurally similar to mind mapping.

If the therapist realizes that the person seeking help is happy about specific events in their life, he can delve deeper, by asking, for instance: "How did you feel at the time?," "How did that happen?," "Which people were present?," "Who knows about the event?" The goal of asking such open-ended questions is to keep the patient within the resource space for as long as possible. The life overview is hence primarily a form of positive life feedback that can later prove to be a vital resource in the therapy.

Potential Difficulties

Drawing up a life overview generally presents few difficulties. It is important that the counselor take advantage of as many opportunities as possible to activate resources. This can be done by showing interest, paying close attention attention, being precise, and offering paths to deepening the conversation. The intervention may become problematic when, in the light of extremely difficult life conditions, there are barely any positive events present in the overview, for example, in connection with a clinically depressed state. However, even in such cases, positive events within the different areas (education, family, relationships) can still usually be found and allow for deeper discussion. Central to this context is that the counselor recognize resources as such and lead the conversation in that direction by showing interest and consistency.

Further Reading

Petzold, H., & Orth, I. (1993). Therapy diaries, life panorama, panorama of health and illness in integrative therapy. *Integrative Therapie, 19*, 95–153.

3.2 Genograms and Ecograms from a Resource Perspective

From a resource perspective, the genogram brings the interpersonal resources from the family's past to the forefront. A genogram usually records family relationships over several generations, including relationships, problematic family events, and fortunes as well as illnesses, births, and deaths. A genogram offers, in compressed form, an overview of all the problematic events from family history and a person's specific biography.

Procedure

Unlike the usual procedure taken when drawing up genograms, where problems lie in the focus, here it is the family's resources that are the central aspect. The perspective covers several generations, going back at least to the grandparents (see Figure 3-1). This procedure allows for a comprehensive resource search within the family systems together with the patient/client. Over the course of preparing the genogram, the roles and the relationships within the family become clear. Particularly important are the relationships in which the patient felt protected and understood. Individual family members can also become examples for the patient to follow and thus valuable role

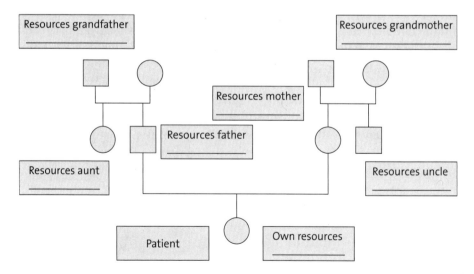

Figure 3-1. Genogram from a resource perspective.

models. In that respect, perceived attractiveness and closeness to the model as well as the value of the resource play vital roles.

The following questions can serve as central questions:
– Whom were you particularly fond of as a child?
– Which of your mother's/father's skills do you particularly appreciate?
– What positive things have you learned from your father/mother?
– What life skills did your family impart to you?
– What resources did your relatives possess?
– What positive myths or stories are there about your family?
– Is there a family treasure?

An ecogram (Hartman, 1995), on the other hand, allow us to visualize social connections that reach beyond the immediate family. Social networks and social perspectives are taken into consideration, allowing for further systems to be included in the activation of resources.

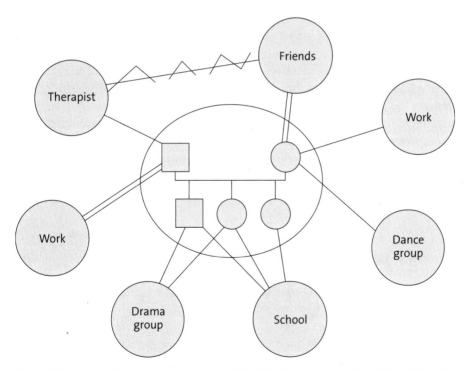

Figure 3-2. Ecogram from a resource perspective, with the current core family (oval circle in the middle) and the extended social context.

Potential Difficulties

Not unlike a genogram, an ecogram consists of highly emotional content. In addition to the immediate use for the client, all other relevant helper systems are recorded on the ecogram. The realization alone that social resources exist inevitably lead to an improvement of the patient's well-being by counteracting the loneliness patients often feel. Unlike a genogram, however, an ecogram represents the family embedded in its environment, the aspect of time mostly being left out of the equation because an ecogram usually refers to the present situation (see Figure 3-2). Potential difficulties in focusing on the family's resources when drawing up a genogram may arise when working with survivors of incest and other forms of abuse within the family. Certainly, with such patients, it is vital to validate their suffering and to not minimize the abuse in any way. At the same time, in later stages of therapy with such patients, after a solid working alliance has already been firmly established, it can be useful to turn to possible strengths, resources, and loved parts of the family and even the abuser after the survivor's suffering has been validated. If nothing else, the very fact that the patient survived the abuse can be framed as revealing internal resources and strength. In addition, even if the survivor is not willing to consider positive aspect of the abuser, in many cases the patient will be able to identify one or more family members with whom he/she had a generally trusting and caring relationship and these relationships can be focused on when focusing on the family's resources. A genogram clearly includes past experiences and emphasizes the patient's personal learning history and family system. Sometimes groups can be a vital resource to the patient, in which case sociograms drawn up from a resource perspective can be used.

Further Reading

Hartman, A. (1995). Dynamic assessment of family relationships. *Families in Society, 76*, 111–122.

McGoldrick, G. (2008). *Genograms. assessments and interventions*. New York: W.W. Norton.

3.3 Miracle Questions and Target Visions

Resource-activating therapy broadens the scope of action which patients or clients can structure; it is hence a form of goal-oriented psychotherapy. This kicks off a process that starts with a target vision. Once the counselor feels that he or she knows enough about the problem, a change of perspective can be initiated.

Procedure

Before asking the miracle questions, the therapist or counselor should prepare the patient for it, e.g., "I'd like to ask you a slightly unusual question ... if that's OK with you. (...) I'd like to ask you – before I move on to the question – even if this question may seem a bit bizarre – to answer it as precisely as as you can. You might feel as if you can't answer it at all. But I'd like you to give it a try anyway. Are you OK with that?" Asking the patient for permission prepares them for an intervention. The patient is given the opportunity to influence the course of the conversation, making counseling or therapy a mutual process. Miracle questions can be asked in different ways, but they should always relate to the patients' experience. A few examples:

- "Let's assume that tonight, while you're asleep, a miracle happens, and the problems you're discussing here are all solved. But because you're asleep you don't know that a miracle has occurred. Tomorrow morning, however, after getting up, you realize something's changed. What could that be? What would you notice? When would you realize that the miracle has happened? What would you do? What would indicate to other people that something has changed?"
- "You go on a trip round the world. During the journey, which takes you to all corners of the world, to your surprise three events you've been wishing for for a long time occur. How would you feel after the events? What has happened? What is different afterward? What is missing while the events are going on? What is the impact of the events on your problems?"
- "Imagine you meet a fairy godmother. She offers you the opportunity to strip away three of your current problems. When you wake the next morning, the problems are gone. What would change? Who would first notice it? How would others react to the change? What would you do and what would be different now?"

- "Most people wish for specific things: 'If I could, only once, get what I want, I'd ...' What would you do if only once you could get what you wanted? Feel free to be unrealistic. What are your wishes, what images or events do you picture in your mind's eye when you imagine a moment of unadulterated joy? What would be happening? Are other people there? What is your reaction? What is their reaction? How did the whole thing start – before the event occurred? Think of it: Every journey starts with the first step outside your own door. What would your first step look like?"
- "On TV, they are planning a piece about you. It will introduce you to a broader audience. What would it say about you? What would other people think of the piece? What would viewers think of your life (exciting, quiet, dramatic)? What would other people say about your life, and how would you feel about that?"
- "Imagine we meet again in 5 years' time. Your life has gone exactly the way you were hoping it would. You've solved the problems you're here for today to your complete satisfaction. You could say you're in a situation where you feel completely at ease. What would you appear like to me? How would your life have changed in the meantime? How did the change occur? What would such a situation look like?"

Miracle questions can be adapted to suit the patient's individual preferences. Depending on what basic needs are relevant to them at this point in time, the miracle question can be asked in connection with a specific need.

With the help of miracle questions the patient can work out a global target vision. In the subsequent processing phase it is important to delineate the vision more clearly. The patient should draw up a plan on how to approximate the target vision: The vision serves as a signpost, and the plan supports the material implementation of the goals aimed for. Placing visions in a hierarchy of goals, partial goals, and micro-goals can prove useful. Micro-goals are goals the person can immediately start implementing in daily life without building new behavioral patterns: They take, as it were, micro-steps in the right direction.

Possible questions for delineating the target visions:
- What would it be like if the problem didn't exist any more?
- What would you notice first?
- Who besides yourself would first notice that the problem is gone – and how would they notice?

Fulfilling these goals should be possible over the course of the therapy. As a rule, one should think in terms of micro-steps. The therapist should always discuss together with the patient whether the goals are realistic. Eventually the patient should receive instructions that are as precise as possible as to how to go about achieving those goals.

Potential Difficulties

Big and important-sounding words such as visions, miracles, or life goals may be perceived as hyperbolic. As mentioned above, the introduction should suit the person's life situation. It is helpful and beneficial if the counselor adopts the patient's language and includes individual images, words, or expressions in the miracle questions. A business manager has a "clear" idea, develops the "perfect project" in a "think tank." "Fairies" and "magicians" are clearly allowed only when they are part of the person's life situation.

Further Reading

Kanfer, F.H., Reinecker, H., & Schmelzer, D. (1991). *Self-management therapy. A textbook for clinical practice.* Champaign, IL: University of Illinois, Department of Psychology.

Willutzki, U., & Koban, C. (2004). Enhancing motivation for psychotherapy: the elaboration of positive perspectives (EPOS). In W.M. Cox & E. Kinger (Eds.), *Handbook of motivational counseling. Concepts, approaches and assessments.* West Sussex: Wiley.

3.4 Other People as Resource Models

Other people are useful as examples when they are accepted as role models and when they possess skills that are useful to the patient. At the same time, the model behavior derived from the role model should not be too far removed to avoid the patient perceiving it as unattainable.

Procedure

This kind of intervention starts with the following central questions:
- Do you know someone who possesses exactly those resources that would be necessary to you in a specific context?
- How does that person behave in similar situations?
- What do they do differently?
- Have you ever behaved similarly to your role model?
- What would others in your life, such as your partner, say?
- When did you ever behave in a similar way to your role model?

The patient/client should experience their resources in an unmediated way: They should not talk about skills and talent without activating them in their natural context. It is therefore necessary for the patient to get a clear idea of the role model's resources. The following interventions can contribute to delineating the resource activation:
- Imagine the situation. Take on your model's role. What would be your thoughts? What feelings would arise in you?
- What do you expect would happen?
- What feelings is this expectation tied to?
- What can you see?
- What are you focusing your attention on?
- What words and sentences would you utter now?
- What would you do now?

Doing "homework" is also useful to experiment and practice the behavior. The patient should try to behave similarly to their role model. When assessing the homework the counselor can ask the following questions:
- What did you do in that situation?
- What was going through your head as you were behaving like that?
- How did you feel in that situation?

- What affected you afterward?
- What were the consequences of your behavior?
- Did something about your attitude change?

Potential Difficulties

One of the main difficulties is that patients make demands on themselves they cannot live up to. Thus, when deciding on the homework, the therapist or counselor has to make sure that the patients do not set unrealistic tasks for themselves. The behavioral goal should be achievable. Micro-steps are again the key. Better to take a micro-step than not to take a giant one.

Further Reading

Bandura, A. (1986). *Social foundations of thought and action: Social cognitive theory.* Englewood Cliffs, NJ: Prentice Hall. Englewood Cliffs, NJ: Prentice Hall.

3.5 Activating Coping Resources Through Role Reversal

The following intervention works well when the patient is ready to face the problem or when the problem seems to have reached a dead end: The patient and therapist swap roles, turning the patient into his or her own counselor. The role reversal allows patients to distance themselves from their own situation, which makes them activate their own solution competencies.

Procedure

Role reversal can be developed out of the therapeutic process without having to invest too much effort. For instance, "I am under the impression that the situation has become stuck. I'd like to understand that more clearly. Would you care to describe the problem more clearly?" The therapist works out the the patient's central thoughts, emotions, and behaviors in the problem situation until they feel they can describe those behaviors, thoughts, and emotions in detail. The therapist now repeats the central thoughts and emotions and describes the behaviors that are part of the problem situation. Subsequently, he or she asks the patient if it is OK to deal with this situation in more detail: "Are you OK with our dealing with this in more detail?" If the patient does agree, the therapist can continue the intervention as described below. One advantage of the exercise is how simple it is to integrate it into the process. Role play enables a high degree of emotional activation, and at the same time, the patient's solution and coping competencies are also activated. The patient is freed from their role as the bearer of the problem. In addition, the intervention serves as an ideal link between coping with the problem and activating resources – and it is a good example of how those two components can be interwoven in the clinical process to achieve the desired effect. The process is described in its entirety below.

1. Exploring the problem situation: moving from the situation to the emotion and cognition;
2. Summarizing and working out: the nagging thought as the central element and possibly an indication as to how convinced the patient is thereof;
3. Asking permission to deal with the problem in more detail;
4. Role reversal: For role reversal it can be useful for the therapist and patient to physically swap seats, which makes taking over the new role easier. "Imagine a friend relates the following problem …" The therapist takes on the

patient's role and describes the difficulties and problems the patient has been talking about. While doing so, the counselor tries to communicate the central cognitions and emotions connected with the experience of the problem situation, which potentially can be condensed into a central statement. As far as possible the therapist should use the patient's own language. After the counselor's describing the problem in the role of the patient, the patient asks him or her questions in the role of the counselor: "How would you respond to that?" Instead of a partner, other close others can be introduced – a brother, a sister, or a work colleague. Who is chosen depends on the individual case. Merely picturing that other person having a similar problem can sometimes be a relief in itself.

5. Checking the viability: test the viability of the suggestions through careful objection, not necessarily by immediately accepting the first suggestion, but by allowing for ambivalence, exposing target conflicts, not disrupting the solution. Tread carefully and "immunize" through a careful "yes-but" game.

6. Returning to the old roles: The seats are reswapped, and both persons return to their original roles. The therapist can now query about the role reversal: " As counselor you just suggested a few strong potential solutions. Do some of the suggestions you made apply to you as well?" The therapist can now work things out by pointing to changes emerging from the role reversal. Attitudes may have changed, convictions questioned, alternative behaviors suggested; or they could be complementary thoughts and newly perceived emotions.

7. Finally, the therapist can ask: "How sure are you at the moment of the original central sentence?"

Potential Difficulties

While clinical practice shows that the exercise can activate numerous fears in the therapist, it can still usually be carried out very well. One difficulty may be that the patient categorically refuses the role reversal. A resource-oriented response to this behavior could be: "You can always say what you want to do and what you don't want to do, this is a vital skill. We can deal with the problem in another way."

A second difficulty may arise over time if the patient cannot think of any alternative ideas while in the role of the counselor. Patients might fail to find solutions as long as they consider themselves uniquely abnormal. In that case the therapist can try to amplify the appeal for help in the role of the patient, which then often activates ideas for solutions.

Clinical experience shows that patients who embrace the intervention also develop helpful ideas for solutions in the role of the counselor.

Further Reading

Greenberg, L.S. (2001). *Emotion-focused therapy: Coaching clients to work through their feelings.* Washington: American Psychological Association

3.6 Planning Pleasure

The larger aim of the interventions discussed in this chapter is to boost pleasant sensations and to activate them as perception. The question is whether pleasure can in fact be learned or trained at all. Pleasure "training" implies not only the pleasure itself, but also some amount of effort, which would seem to be the opposite of something enjoyable. Below we do not deal with how to heighten the ability to feel pleasure; rather we invite you to follow the individual tracks that lead to the experience of pleasant sensations. Sensitizing the patient's senses seeks to create positive experiences that run counter to those he experiences at the beginning of the therapy.

Procedure

– *Planning pleasure:* Consciousness is a precondition to learning how to feel pleasure again – in other words, conscious pleasure. The patient/client should have the time and opportunity to direct his or her attention to feeling pleasure. In order to create the proper spatial and situational conditions necessary for pleasure, one usually has to have a plan: The time and the situation have to be created. What can be enjoyed and how it is enjoyed depends more on the patient's experiential background. Normally, it can be assumed that people can reflect back on enjoyable experiences they have had in their lifetimes. It is useful to refer to those. The first step for the patient is to learn that pleasure is preceded by a phase in which pleasure is set up, in which one actively creates the conditions that are relevant to having an enjoyable experience. This preparation phase is not only a necessary precondition, it can become enjoyable in and of itself. The boundary between the preparation and the start of the actual pleasure is at best blurred.
– *Time and duration:* The time for experiencing the enjoyable action and how long it is to last has to be planned. Often people say that they do not have the time to enjoy themselves. This is the crux of the matter: They hinder themselves in doing so. This is not an argument against pleasure as such, but rather underlines the importance of effectively planning pleasure. Not only when patients are to enjoy themselves should be considered, but also how long, i.e., that there is also an end to the enjoyable event.

Potential Difficulties

What is pleasant? What does a person perceive as pleasurable? Many actions may be deemed pleasurable because they are accompanied by pleasant thoughts or feelings. With clinically depressed patients, this point is inextricably tied to the vicious circle of depression. Events or changes perceived by the patient in the past as pleasant can offer a clue to enjoyable actions.

If the patient primarily mentions passive behavior when asked about pleasant actions, e.g., watching TV, it is vital to determine the attendant thoughts and feelings. Of course, watching TV is a perfectly enjoyable activity; however, if a depressed patient watches TV with the thought: "Here I am again in front of the TV, that's boring. All I do is slouch around ...," then that is certainly not pleasurable. Whether something is enjoyable or not can be checked against the thoughts and sensations of the person. This check is important if the preparation of the enjoyable action is to lead to something that is in fact enjoyable.

The therapist should try to find out together with the patient what is pleasurable. Possible questions are:

– What kind of pleasure is allowed and what kind isn't allowed?
– What do you like right now?
– What can you imagine achieving?
– Are there areas that you picture as being pleasant, but haven't delved into yet?

What is good and what is not good comes down to the patient. In that sense, it is important to know what is pleasant, but it is equally important to know what is unpleasant and what the person does not want.

What Does it Mean to "Really Enjoy" Something?

It is important to communicate to the patient that there is no right or wrong about pleasure. Pleasure exercises can lead to experiences that are more or less pleasant. Learning to feel pleasure means practicing to feel pleasure. One cannot *not* feel pleasure. All people can differentiate between pleasant and unpleasant sensations. When feeling pleasure, it is important to locate those sensations that are pleasant and thus steer toward having more pleasant than unpleasant experiences.

If pleasure becomes a taboo, experiencing pleasure can become very difficult. Sexuality, for instance, is a taboo area to many people. The extent to which pleasure is accepted or forbidden is highly dependent on one's family history. Family upbringing is the first normative authority that imparts how and where something can be perceived as pleasurable – or not. Rigid family rules can inhibit the perception of pleasurable sensations.

Further Reading

Lutz, R. (1983). *Therapy theory for the promotion of joyful experiencing and action.* Stuttgart: Beltz.

3.7 Resource Activation Through Imaginative Procedures

In order to improve the patient's well-being, relaxation techniques can be helpful. In many cases, a change in the patient's level of tension and an increase in their well-being can be achieved in a short time. Choose a method that suits the patient's individual preconditions, for example, relaxation exercises from the progressive muscle relaxation technique, hypnotherapy, or imaginative procedures. The procedure we look into in more detail below is based on the imagination method.

Imaginative procedures allow the therapist to use images during relaxation in order to enhance the patient's mood and to directly activate their positive emotions.

Procedure

Introducing a patient to an imagination exercise might look something like this:

> "I'd now like to try out a little exercise with you. It's a relaxation exercise. Some of this may feel unfamiliar, but remember it is just an offer: You can't do anything right or wrong. If you feel like it, you can choose to stop the exercise at any moment. However, it's possible that some of the instructions might in fact work for you, and you'll want to follow them. You might notice that certain objects or certain images help you relax, whereas others may not. Just follow those aspects of the exercise that help you relax. Perhaps you don't feel any noticeable relaxation, in which case just be open to what is happening. That doesn't mean that you've done something wrong. Our experiences with relaxation exercises show that everyone has an individual reaction to them. Are you ready to begin? Do you have any questions? OK, well, let's start, then."

The exercise should not be too long; for some patients this kind of exercise is completely new, and they might feel insecure about it. The first attempt at imagination or relaxation exercises should last no longer than 15 minutes. If the patient experiences the exercise as positive, a longer imagination exercise may be carried out in a follow-up session. Once the patient is receptive, the therapist can start the imagination exercise. Talk slowly and make sure there are enough pauses.

A Place of Quietude and Strength

Find a comfortable position and try to relax as best you can. Find a position and a spot in this room that will allow you to really relax. You might want to change the position of the chair, you might want to sit or lie down. Your gaze can be directed in the room or out the window. Try out what is the most comfortable position for you. Take your time. Sometimes you think you've found the right position, but suddenly you feel the impulse to change your position again. Give yourself permission to do so. The change may be big or small, maybe only the position of your feet or hands, head or neck. Sometimes a small movement can in fact help the body relax further. Allow your body to find the position where it can continue relaxing further and further. Even after a while you may realize that a certain posture or position isn't as comfortable as you initially thought. Feel free to change it again. Your body will find a position in which it feels entirely comfortable. Try and make everything around you unimportant. Dismiss for a short while all objects, words, events that previously seemed so very important so that you can get in touch with yourself. Notice how the air is flowing into your body and back out, how your breath carries you. Notice it but without changing anything, the way your body takes care of you, breath after breath. If you want to, close your eyes and focus on yourself, on your own breathing. The air flows in and out, just like that, by itself. Maybe there's a short pause after each breath – allow it: It is your body recovering. And while you're lying or sitting there and relaxing further and further, pictures may begin to appear before your mind's eye. At first maybe it's just dots, patterns, or colors. Images. The images might stay a while or go away again. They might be sharp or blurred. Maybe they change or morph. Just allow what is happening in your mind's eye to happen. You may be surprised at all the things you can see with your eyes closed. Maybe one of the images is particularly pleasurable. Try and stay with it, look at it. Notice where you are. Who else is there? Is there a specific smell? Or taste? An event or situation, maybe it's inside or outside? Is it warm or cold? Maybe you can feel the temperature on your skin. Look around you and absorb the image. Seeing, smelling, tasting, hearing, feeling. Taking it all in with all your senses, notice it and savor it.

Enjoy the pleasurable and agreeable feeling of energy and relaxation. Of just being here and taking in this place of quietude, strength, and relaxation. Feel it and let it affect you. Enjoy it and absorb it, the energy and strength. Take something with you from this place, like a souvenir from a trip. Then you can go back anytime you want.

And now slowly say good-bye to this place, notice how the air is still flowing into your body and back out, just like that. Take all the time you need to come back to here, to this room. Allow your body to take what it needs, maybe you want to stretch, run your hands across your face. To be here again in this room and open your eyes.

Potential Difficulties

When assessing the exercise afterward, it is important to process what the patient has experienced during it. The therapist should remain open to the patient's experiences. With a patient who says that they couldn't really get into the exercise, it is important that the therapist emphasize the patient's active contributions, for instance, that they didn't resist it, or that they tried to actively do the exercise. It is important to evaluate even this experience in depth. The therapist may want to point out the subjectivity of the experience. If patients denigrate themselves, thinking "I can't do this," the following explanation may prove helpful: "I think you actively embraced this new exercise. If you feel now that you can't do this, this might just have to do with the fact that it is something new and is unfamiliar to you. And it's perfectly normal not to know how to do unfamiliar things. It's like sports: Remember what it was like when you first stood on skis. You probably were a bit unsteady on your feet. Relaxation is very similar. But if you're interested in it and you try and relax regularly, you will notice over time that you can experience new and different things."

With this exercise, as with all other interventions described in this manual, it is important that the therapist emphasize the patient's active contributions in order to give them a sense of their own activity. The therapist should, whenever possible, enable the client to become more aware of their own "actions." Whenever the client gains a better sense of their own activity, they also become more aware of their own resources.

Practice makes perfect, as the old saying goes. The therapist should encourage the patient to do the relaxation exercise on their own before the next session. You may want to give the patient a taped recording of it.

Further Reading

Singer, J.L., & Pope K.S. (Eds.). (1978). *The power of human imagination*. New York: Plenum.

3.8 Resource Diary

The function of diaries, among other things, is to identify relationships the person may only vaguely be aware of and whose signposts are not clearly recognizable. In the treatment of depression, for instance, a diary may demonstrate the relationship between positive events and positive moods. Structured resource diaries can refer to broader areas, including social support, individual skills and talents, i.e., all areas with potential resource hotspots (Chapter 1) and resource perspectives (Chapter 2.1–2.6). These could be specific thematic areas that are dealt with in more depth in the therapy or a more broader focus to highlight events that would normally be deemed unimportant or negligible.

Procedure

The choice of resource areas has to be made so as to monitor everyday events:

1) Define the resource areas to be documented in the following week;
2) Define a response format (e.g., situation, event, mood, personal resource).

Potential Difficulties

The areas monitored have to be specific enough to be useful within the individual case formulation. The focus should hence not be placed on what the individual is already aware of, but rather on what is located in the gray area of the semiconscious. Criticism along the lines of "Oh, I understand all that" can be countered by pointing out that a full understanding of unproblematic areas can be helpful in understanding problematic aspects.

3.9 Differentiating Between Positive Feelings and Moods

At a high level of abstraction, affective experience can be placed in one of two categories – positive or negative affect. Patients often generalize their emotional state in strongly abstract terms and even upon repeated questioning hardly ever differentiate ("Today I'm just great!" or "Last week I felt like crap!"). Traditionally, psychotherapy and counseling have been geared to understanding the generation of negative affect (e.g., by means of situational analysis, an in-depth review, or the discovery of automatic negative thoughts). But these methods can also be applied with a view toward discovering positive experience, with the goal being to become more aware of positive affective experience.

Procedure

Worksheet 3 allows one to become aware of and to gain an overview of the spectrum of positive feeling. Collating different situations from the recent and distant past connected to a specific positive mood serves to emphasize the quality and strength of positive experience. Not only highly intense "one-off" events are of significance; everyday events have to be considered as well. Using mood questionnaires can sharpen a patient's awareness of current mood.

Potential Difficulties

The person may remembers only situations from the distant past and regret not experiencing such things any more. If this is the case, it is vital to look for situations that enable the person to experience positive affects in their everyday life – even if only to a small degree.

Further Reading

Fitzpatrick, M.R., & Stalikas, A. (2008). Positive emotions in psychotherapy. *Journal of Psychotherapy Integration, 18,* 155–233.

Rashid, T. (2009). Positive interventions in clinical practice. *Journal of Clinical Psychology*, doi: 10.10002/jclp.20588

3.10 Reframing and Normalization

The effect of positive reassessment (reframing) and normalization on a specific person or target group is as specific and cultural as a good joke. The aim of reframing is to make problems more manageable – to qualify and to contain them. Reframings can come in the shape of metaphors, stories, and allegories. The insurmountable problems the patient faces can thereby lose some of their menace and complexity. Usually situations may be found in a person's biography in which the problem behavior they have acquired was useful or even crucial to their survival. Problem behavior is hence not inherently problematic, but merely applied at the wrong time. The way events are perceived as well as their attendant attitudes and value systems make up the individual way of absorbing and processing information. Nearly every problem has its good sides. The aim of reframing is for the patient to re-evaluate things: to allow for the problem to be accessed from its positive angle. A patient seeing previous behavior as exclusively problematic can now detect a new meaning to the behavior with the help of such reassessments. It is not just irrational, as the patient used to think, but now can be read within a specific situational context to have certain effects – and mostly positive ones at that. The patient is often amazed at such reassessments. Reframing is a question of the specific therapy situation, particularly the therapy style. It cannot be divorced from clear therapeutic convictions and an intention on the part of the therapist to see the patient from his or her most positive side.

Procedure

It can be helpful to set up a card index of possible reframings tailored to the target group. Table 3-1 gives a few examples of common reframings and normalizations. Try and add positive synonyms to negative attributes with the help of the word thesaurus when you're working on the concept for a case or a case report – and then reread your report!

Of course, some events can't be reframed in a few words, but need the help of metaphors:

– Therapy can sometimes be like a mountain hike: We travel together, but you have to walk on your own.
– School, training, or studies are like a marathon: Being head of the class in year 1 is not enough; you need to have the stamina to stick it out till the end.

Table 3-1. Possible reframings and normalizations

Problem aspect	Reframe into	Positive behavior
Sensitive	→	Alert, attentive
Fearful	→	Being concerned about yourself, only those who are afraid need a lot of courage
Withdrawn	→	Considerate, discreet
Envious	→	Knowing what you want
Jealous	→	Protecting the source of one's own relationship needs
Arrogant	→	Knowing how to maintain distance
Confused	→	Realizing that there are many possibilities out there
Aggressive	→	Fighting for your own goals
Pigheaded	→	Self-assertive and self-confident
Worthless	→	Nothing is without value
Depressed	→	Melancholy can suggest deep understanding
Mistrustful	→	Careful
Tense	→	Full of energy
Docile	→	Being open to compromise
Hurt	→	Time for healing
Vulnerable	→	We're all vulnerable
Sensitive	→	Being able to empathize

- If you roll a 1 three times in a row, it is (mathematically) unfair, of course, but in the end it might turn out to be a blessing …
- You don't want to change depending on the game. OK, just try it.

Potential Difficulties

Reframings tell you what the counselor is thinking and how far the clients are willing to go down the road toward reassessment. Reframings are thus also always shaped by one's perception and the therapist's own background. Nevertheless, the aim of reframing is to obtain a better, more complete patient's understanding of oneself. It can be helpful if the therapist adopts some of the patient's images, words, and metaphors.

Further Reading

De Shazer (1988). *Clues. Investigating solutions in brief therapy*. New York: Norton.
Walter, J.L., & Peller, J.E. (1992). *Becoming solution-focused in brief therapy*. New York: Brunner/Mazel.

Appendix

- *Worksheet 1.* Resource Priming
- *Worksheet 2.* Resource-Oriented Dialog Strategies – Possible Questions
- *Worksheet 3.* Differentiating Positive Feelings and Moods

Worksheet 1. Resource priming

Resource hotspots		How can it be activated?		How strongly was the resource activated?				
Test battery/clinical impression	Important	Within therapy	Outside of therapy	Session 1	Session 2	Session 3	Session 4	Session 5
1								
2								
3								
4								
5								
Further resources over the course of the therapy								

How strongly was the resource activated? 4 = extremely; 3 = very; 2 = fairly; 1 = somewhat; 0 = not at all.

From: Flückiger, C., Wüsten, G., Zinbarg, R.E., & Wampold, B.E. *Resource Activation – Using Clients' Own Strengths in Psychotherapy and Counseling.*
© Hogrefe Publishing 2010.

Worksheet 2. Resource-oriented dialog strategies – possible questions

1) Perceiving and validating directly available resources – Have I honored the unproblematic results of a questionnaire? – Have I properly strengthened behavior that is useful to the therapy? – What difference does the patient's coming to therapy make?	vs.	Actively introducing unused resources – Does the patient have skills that were forgotten in the actual situation? – Does the patient have skills he or she does not dare to use yet? – Is a step in the right direction being made?
2) Verbalizing resources – Can I picture the resource the patient is describing to me? – Have I understood the subjective significance of the resource for the person? – What does the person's "beaming" mean when they tell a story?	vs.	Making resources immediately experienceable – What brings joy to the patient and can I integrate this into the process? – How can I adapt the therapy process to suit the patient's skills? – Do I adapt the therapy process to the patient's "environment" (language, metaphors, nonverbal cues)?
3) Strengthening personal resources – What is the patient passionate about? – What does the person feel committed to? – What leaves the patient cold? And why?	vs.	Boosting the resources of the social network – Are there strong role models in their family or circle of friends? – In what areas can the patient count on social support? – Is there someone the patient trusts?
4) Picking up existing or unused skills and talents (potential resources) – What is the person particularly good at? – What comes natural to them? – When does the person begin to "flow"?	vs.	Integrating existing goals and desires (motivational resources) – What dreams does the patient nurture? – What idols does the person have? – In what areas does the person have positive expectations of change?

5) Focusing on problem-independent resources	vs.	Taking advantage of problem-relevant resources
– In what areas does the patient perceive themselves as being competent?		– To what extent can the problem be defined?
– Were there good times in the past?		– Are there exceptions?
– Did I make time to allow the patient to rave about their passions?		– What is the effect of the improvements that have occurred?
		– To what extent can I validate the understanding of the problem?
6) Optimizing usable resources	vs.	Maintaining trainable resources
– To what extent can a resource be exhausted?		– Have I repeated the results enough?
– What are the limits of a usable resource?		– Is regularity useful?
– What is means-ends relationship?		– Is there any potential for variation?

From: Flückiger, C., Wüsten, G., Zinbarg, R.E., & Wampold, B.E. *Resource Activation – Using Clients' Own Strengths in Psychotherapy and Counseling.*
© Hogrefe Publishing 2010.

Worksheet 3. Differentiating positive feelings and moods

Feeling/mood	Magnitude	Situation							
Cheerful, happy									
Untroubled									
Excited, euphoric									
Relaxed, calm									
Longing, enraptured									
Optimistic									
Proud									
Active									
Alert									

Feeling/mood	Magnitude	Situation
Interested		
Decisive		
...		
...		
...		

Magnitude: 1 = slightly; 2 = noticeable; 3 = pronounced; 4 = strong; 5 = maximum level.

Bibliography

Bandura, A. (1986). *Social foundations of thought and action: Social cognitive theory.* Englewood Cliffs, NJ: Prentice Hall.

De Shazer (1988). *Clues. Investigating solutions in brief therapy.* New York: Norton.

Duckworth, A.L., Steen, T.A., & Seligman, M.E.P. (2005). Positive psychology in clinical practice. *Annual Review of Clinical Psychology, 1,* 629–651.

Fitzpatrick, M.R., & Stalikas, A. (2008). Positive emotions in psychotherapy. *Journal of Psychotherapy Integration, 18,* 155–233.

Flückiger, C., Caspar, F., Grosse Holtforth, M., & Willutzki, U. (2009). Working with the patients' strengths: A microprocess approach. *Psychotherapy Research, 19,* 213–223.

Flückiger, C., & Grosse Holtforth, M. (2008). Focusing the therapist's attention on the patient's strengths – A preliminary study to foster a mechanism of change in out-patient psychotherapy. *Journal of Clinical Psychology, 64,* 876–890.

Gassmann, D., & Grawe, K. (2006). General change mechanisms. The relation between problem activation and resource activation in successful and unsuccessful therapeutic interactions. *Journal of Clinical Psychology and Psychotherapy, 13,* 1–11.

Grawe, K. (1997). Research-informed psychotherapy. *Psychotherapy Research, 7,* 1–19.

Grawe, K. (2004). *Psychological therapy.* Seattle, WA: Hogrefe.

Grawe, K. (2006). *Neuropsychotherapy.* Mahwah, NJ: Erlbaum.

Greenberg, L.S. (2001). *Emotion-focused therapy: Coaching clients to work through their feelings.* Washington, DC: American Psychological Association.

Gollwitzer, P.M., & Schaal, B. (2001). How goals and plans affect action. In S. Messick & J.M. Collis (Eds.), *Intelligence and personality: Bridging the gap in theory and measurement* (pp. 139–161). Mahwah, NJ: Erlbaum.

Groner, R., Groner, M., & Bischof, W.F. (1983). *Methods of heuristics.* Hillsdale, NJ: Erlbaum.

Hartman, A. (1995). Dynamic assessment of family relationships. *Families in Society, 76,* 111–122.

Howard, K.I., Lueger, R.J., Maling, M.S., & Martinovich, Z. (1993). A phase model of psychotherapy outcome: Causal mediation of change. *Journal of Consulting an Clinical Psychology, 61,* 678–685.

Kanfer, F.H., Reinecker, H., & Schmelzer, D. (1991). *Self-management therapy. A textbook for clinical practice.* Champaign, IL: University of Illinois, Department of Psychology.

Lutz, R. (1983). *Therapy theory for the promotion of joyful experiencing and action.* Stuttgart: Beltz.

McGoldrick, G. (2008). *Genograms. assessments and interventions.* New York: W.W. Norton.

Petzold, H., & Orth, I. (1993). Therapy diaries, life panorama, panorama of health and illness in integrative therapy. *Integrative Therapie, 19*, 95–153.

Rashid, T. (2009). Positive interventions in clinical practice. *Journal of Clinical Psychology*, DOI 10.10002/jclp.20588

Rosenhan, D.L. (1973). On being sane in insane places. *Science, 179*, 250–258.

Singer, J.L., & Pope K.S. (Eds.). (1978). *The power of human imagination*. New York: Plenum.

Smith, E., & Grawe, K. (2003). What makes psychotherapy sessions productive? A new approach to bridging the gap between process research and practice. *Clinical Psychology and Psychotherapy, 10*, 275–285.

Smith, E., & Grawe, K. (2005). Which therapeutic mechanisms works when? A step toward the formulation of empirically validated guidelines for therapists' session-to-session decisions. *Clinical Psychology and Psychotherapy, 12*, 112–123.

Walter, J.L., & Peller, J.E. (1992). *Becoming solution-focused in brief therapy*. New York: Brunner/Mazel

Willutzki, U., & Koban, C. (2004). Enhancing motivation for psychotherapy: The elaboration of positive perspectives (EPOS). In W.M. Cox & E. Kinger (Eds.), *Handbook of motivational counseling. Concepts, approaches and assessments*. West Sussex: Wiley.

Index

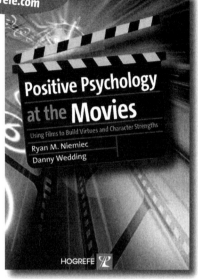